Ex Libris

End Papers from *Oeuvres de Molière*
Paris, Lefilleul Librairie, 1881
10¾ x 7¼ inches
William A. Sargent Collection
Book Reg. 2750

THE BOOK LOVER'S
Book of Lists

Twenty Lists of
Books Too Good to Miss

MUSEUM OF FINE ARTS,
BOSTON

First published in 1994 by the
Museum of Fine Arts, Boston
Department of Retail Publications
295 Huntington Avenue
Boston, Massachusetts 02115

ISBN 0-87846-416-6

Designed by Dennis O'Reilly, Ars Agassiz

Cover and title page (detail)
John George Brown
American, 1831–1913
Girl by the Seacoast
Oil on canvas
25 x 17⅛ inches (63.5 x 43.5 cm.)
Gift in Part of Walstein C. Findlay, Jr.,
in Memory of William Wadsworth Findlay
61.1294

Color separation and printing by Sfera - Milano
Printed in Italy

To the many librarians and booksellers who have contributed their suggestions to the lists of books you'll find here.

Thomas Hart Benton
American, 1889–1975
New England Editor, 1946
Oil and tempera on gesso panel
30 x 37 inches
The Hayden Collection.
46.1456

THE BOOK LOVER'S

Book of Lists

Mary S. Chapin
American, 19th century
Solitude, c. 1820
Watercolor
15¼ x 13⅝ inches
M. and M. Karolik Collection
60.469

"*If you cannot read all your books, at any rate handle, or fondle them. Arrange them on your own plan so that if you do not know what is in them, at least you know where they are.*"

Winston Churchill

Odilon Redon
French, 1840–1916
The Reader (Le Liseur), 1892
Lithograph
12⁵⁄₁₆ x 9³⁄₈ inches
Katherine E. Bullard Fund in Memory of Francis Bullard
1992.21

CONTENTS

INTRODUCTION

Book lovers everywhere are always happy to pass on recommendations of books too good to miss; newspapers and magazines carry enticing reviews of newly published books; annual awards are given to books of outstanding merit. Too often these suggestions for future reading have been forgotten when it's time to stock up on books for long plane trips or vacations. By the time a book is published in paperback, the original inspiring review has been lost and the notes from friends about wonderful new authors or rediscovered classics have vanished.

This book is intended to be a convenient place for book lovers to record notes on titles to remember as well as books already read or purchased. The handy shape makes it easy to carry along on visits to the library or bookstore. The book can also be used to keep a list of books on loan to friends and books given as gifts. Best of all, by adding your own favorites to this book, you will have created a unique gift sure to please any book lover.

The Book Lover's Book of Lists contains hundreds of titles, new and old, arranged in categories that invite browsing. You will find books that appeal to your every reading mood from humor to biography, from science fiction to romance. Each list represents only a small fraction of the number of titles that could be included. The lists are not intended to be comprehensive, but are meant to inspire; we hope that you will discover new authors as well as old favorites and that you will never be without a wonderful new book to read.

John George Brown
American, 1831–1913
Girl by the Seacoast
Oil on canvas
25 x 17⅛ inches (63.5 x 43.5 cm.)
Gift in Part of Walstein C. Findlay, Jr.,
in Memory of William Wadsworth Findlay
61.129+

If you could choose three books to take to a desert island, what would they be? This question elicited lively response at the lunch table at the Museum, where nearly everyone had a favorite book to recommend. You may find your own favorites here plus some unexpected choices.

Kobo Abé *The Woman in the Dune*

Natalie Babbit *Tuck Everlasting*

The Bible

The Boy Scout Handbook

Simone de Beauvoir *She Came to Stay*

Rita Mae Brown *Rubyfruit Jungle*

John Buchan *The Thirty-Nine Steps*

Willa Cather *Death Comes for the Archbishop*

Truman Capote *Breakfast at Tiffanys*

Colette *In My Mother's House*

Daniel Defoe *Robinson Crusoe*

Charles Dickens *A Christmas Carol*

A dictionary

Benjamin Hoff *The Tao of Pooh*

Maxine Kumin *Our Down Time Will Be Brief*

Marjorie Kinnan Rawlings *The Yearling*

Tom Robbins *Even Cowgirls Get the Blues*

Anne Rice *The Witching Hour*

Irma Rombauer *The Joy of Cooking*

Antoine de Saint-Exupery *The Little Prince*

Bram Stoker *Dracula*

Mark Twain *The Adventures of Huckleberry Finn*

Francis Alexander
American, 1800–1880
Charles Dickens
Oil on canvas
44 x 35½ inches
Gift of the Estate of Mrs. James T. Fields
24.18

UNFORGETTABLE CLASSICS

Jane Austen *Pride and Prejudice*

Honoré de Balzac *Père Goriot*

Charlotte Brontë *Jane Eyre*

Emily Brontë *Wuthering Heights*

Stephen Crane *The Red Badge of Courage*

Richard Henry Dana *Two Years before the Mast*

Charles Dickens *David Copperfield*

Feodor Mikhailovich Dostoyevski
The Brothers Karamazov

Alexandre Dumas *The Three Musketeers*

George Eliot *Middlemarch*

Henry Fielding *Tom Jones*

Thomas Hardy *Jude the Obscure*

Nathaniel Hawthorne *The Scarlet Letter*

Victor Hugo *Les Misérables*

Henry James *The Ambassadors*

Herman Melville *Moby Dick*

Marcel Proust *Remembrance of Things Past*

Stendhal *The Red and the Black*

Robert Louis Stevenson *Dr. Jekyll and Mr. Hyde*

Harriet Beecher Stowe *Uncle Tom's Cabin*

Jonathan Swift *Gulliver's Travels*

William Makepeace Thackeray *Vanity Fair*

Henry David Thoreau *Walden*

Leo Tolstoy *War and Peace*

Anthony Trollope *Barchester Towers*

Mark Twain *The Adventures of Huckleberry Finn*

Oscar Wilde *The Picture of Dorian Gray*

Émile Zola *Germinal*

Ce crâne, Monsieur, était celui d'Yorick, le Bouffon du Roi. — Hélas! Pauvre Yorick!

Eugène Delacroix
French, 1798–1843
Hamlet and Horatio in the Graveyard, 1843
Lithograph
11 x 8⅛ inches
Bequest of William P. Babcock
B1239

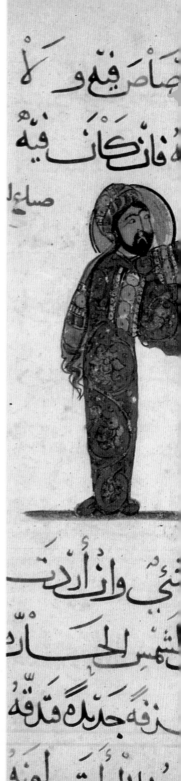

Two Physicians with a Large Jar
Page from an illustrated copy
of *De Materia Medica*
of Pedanius Dioscorodes
Text copied by
'Abdullah ibn al-Fadl
Iraq, probably Bhagdad
A.H. Rabjab 621
(June–July 1924)
Opaque watercolor, ink
and gold on paper
Francis Bartlett Donation of
1912 and Picture Fund
14.536

ثُمَّ أَنَا أَصُبُّ فِيهِ مِلْخًا ثُمَّ حَامِضًا ثُمَّ عَلَقَ ا
لَخَ الخَلِّ ثُمَّ طَنْ فِمِ لَا أَنَا قِرَهُ أَيَّامًا ثُمَّ أَفْحَ خُ

سَتُرَ خًا فَاجْرِدُكَ ثُمَّ اعَلُكَ حَتَّى لَا يَبْقَى مِنْ
عَلَهُ اقْرَصَهُ فَاعْجِنْهُ نُخْلَ حَامِضًا ثُمَّ نَشْهُ فِ
عَانِهُ كُوزِ أَبْيَضٍ بَالِغٍ وَحَرِّقُهُ إِنْ يَأْخُذُ خُ

Edmund Tarbell
American, 1862–1938
Girl Reading, 1909
Oil on canvas
32½ x 28¼ inches
The Hayden Collection
09.209

MEMORABLE MODERN CLASSICS

James Agee *A Death in the Family*

James Baldwin *Go Tell It on the Mountain*

Saul Bellow *The Adventures of Augie March*

Albert Camus *The Stranger*

Willa Cather *My Àntonia*

Theodore Dreiser *Sister Carrie*

Ralph Ellison *The Invisible Man*

William Faulkner *The Sound and the Fury*

Graham Greene *The Quiet American*

Joseph Heller *Catch-22*

Ernest Hemingway *The Old Man and the Sea*

James Joyce *Ulysses*

D. H. Lawrence *Sons and Lovers*

Harper Lee *To Kill a Mockingbird*

Malcolm Lowry *Under the Volcano*

Vladimir Nabokov *Lolita*

George Orwell *Animal Farm*

Walker Percy *The Moviegoer*

J. D. Salinger *The Catcher in the Rye*

John Steinbeck *The Grapes of Wrath*

Evelyn Waugh *Brideshead Revisited*

Max Weber
American, 1881–1961
Three Literary Gentlemen, 1945
Oil on canvas
29¼ x 36 inches
Gift of the William H. Lane Foundation
1990.454

NOTABLE FICTION OF THE 1970s

Donald Barthelme *The Dead Father*

Saul Bellow *Humboldt's Gift*

Dee Brown *Bury My Heart at Wounded Knee*

E. L. Doctorow *Ragtime*

Margaret Craven *I Heard the Owl Call My Name*

Maxine Hong Kingston *The Woman Warrior: Memories of a Girlhood Among Ghosts*

John le Carré *Tinker, Tailor, Soldier, Spy*

Norman Maclean *A River Runs Through It*

V. S. Naipaul *A Bend in the River*

John Nichols *The Milagro Beanfield War*

Michael Ondaatje *Coming Through Slaughter*

Barbara Pym *Quartet in Autumn*

Wallace Stegner *Angle of Repose*

Anne Tyler *Celestial Navigation*

Eudora Welty *The Optimist's Daughter*

NOTABLE FICTION OF THE 1980s

Isabel Allende *The House of the Spirits*

Julian Barnes *Flaubert's Parrot*

Italo Calvino *If on a winter's night a traveler*

Pat Conroy *The Prince of Tides*

Don DeLillo *White Noise*

Pete Dexter *Paris Trout*

Michael Dorris *A Yellow Raft in Blue Water*

Louise Erdrich *Love Medicine: A Novel*

Mark Harris *Bang the Drum Slowly*

Mark Helprin *A Winter's Tale*

Ruth Prawer Jhabvala *Heat and Dust*

Milan Kundera *The Unbearable Lightness of Being*

Bobbie Ann Mason *In Country*

Howard Frank Mosher *A Stranger in the Kingdom*

Marge Piercy *Gone to Soldiers*

NOTABLE FICTION OF THE 1990s

Margaret Atwood *The Robber Bride*

Alice Hoffman *Seventh Heaven*

Barbara Kingsolver *Pigs in Heaven*

Terry McMillan *Waiting to Exhale*

Norman Rush *Mating*

Valerie Sayers *Who Do You Love*

Anne Tyler *Saint Maybe*

John Edgar Wideman *Philadelphia Fire*

Childe Hassam
American, 1859–1935
Lady Reading
Watercolor
19¼ x 12¼ inches
Bequest of Kathleen Rothe
65.1303

RECENT PULITZER PRIZES IN FICTION

1980 Norman Mailer *The Executioner's Song*

1981 John Kennedy Toole *A Confederacy of Dunces*

1982 John Updike *Rabbit Is Rich*

1983 Alice Walker *The Color Purple*

1984 William Kennedy *Ironweed*

1985 Alison Lurie *Foreign Affairs*

1986 Larry McMurtry *Lonesome Dove*

1987 Peter Taylor *A Summons to Memphis*

1988 Toni Morrison *Beloved*

1989 Anne Tyler *Breathing Lessons*

1990 Oscar Hijuelos *The Mambo Kings Play Songs of Love*

1991 John Updike *Rabbit at Rest*

1992 Jane Smiley *A Thousand Acres*

1993 Robert Olen Butler *A Good Scent from a Strange Mountain*

1994 E. Annie Proulx *The Shipping News*

Anonymous
French, 15th century
"Adoration of the Magi"
Book of Hours
Gold and tempera on vellum with leather binding
H: 1.85 cm x W: 1.4 cm x D: .40 cm
Bequest of Mrs. Arthur Croft, Gardner Brewer Collection
01.6751

RECENT BOOKER AWARD WINNERS

1980 William Golding *Rites of Passage*

1981 Salman Rushdie *Midnight's Children*

1982 Thomas Keneally *Schindler's Ark*

1983 J. M. Coetzee *Life & Times of Michael K.*

1984 Anita Brookner *Hotel du Lac*

1985 Keri Hulme *The Bone People*

1986 Kingsley Amis *The Old Devils*

1987 Penelope Lively *Moon Tiger*

1988 Peter Carey *Oscar and Lucinda*

1989 Kazuo Ishiguro *The Remains of the Day*

1990 A. S. Byatt *Possession: A Romance*

1991 Ben Okri *The Famished Road*

1992 Michael Ondaatje *The English Patient*

1992 Barry Unsworth *Sacred Hunger*

1993 Roddy Doyle *Paddy Clarke* Ha Ha Ha

William W. Churchill
American, 1858–1926
Leisure, 1910
Oil on canvas
30⅛ x 25⅛ inches
Gift of Gorham Hubbard
12.325

RECENT PULITZER PRIZES FOR BIOGRAPHY

1980 *The Rise of Theodore Roosevelt*
Edmund Morris

1981 *Peter the Great: His Life and World*
Robert K. Massie

1982 *Grant: A Biography* William S. McFeely

1983 *Growing Up* Russell Baker

1984 *Booker T. Washington* Louis R. Harlan

1985 *The Life and Times of Cotton Mather*
Kenneth Silverman

1986 *Louise Bogan: A Portrait* Elizabeth Frank

1987 *Bearing the Cross: Martin Luther King Jr.
and the Southern Christian Leadership
Conference* David J. Garrow

1988 *Look Homeward: A Life of Thomas Wolfe*
David Herbert Donald

1989 *Oscar Wilde* Richard Ellmann

1990 *Machiavelli in Hell* Sebastian de Grazia

1991 *Jackson Pollock: An American Saga*
Steven Naifeh and Gregory White Smith

1992 *Fortunate Son: The Healing of a Vietnam Vet*
Lewis B. Puller Jr.

1993 *Truman* David McCullough

1994 *W. E. B. DuBois: Biography of a Race,
1868–1919* David Levering Lewis

Aubrey Beardsley
English, 1872–1898
Illustration from Sir Thomas Malory's
Le Morte D'Arthur
London, William Caxton, 1893–94
Woodcut
8⁷/₁₆ x 1³/₈ inches
William A. Sargent Collection
Book Reg. 2390

STRANGE AND PROVOCATIVE OTHER WORLDS

Isaac Asimov *The Foundation Trilogy*

Margaret Atwood *The Handmaid's Tale*

Ray Bradbury *Fahrenheit 451*

Anthony Burgess *A Clockwork Orange*

Robert Heinlein *Stranger in a Strange Land*

Frank Herbert *Dune*

Russell Hoban *Riddley Walker*

Aldous Huxley *Brave New World*

Walter M. Miller Jr. *A Canticle for Liebowitz*

George Orwell *1984*

Thomas Pynchon *Gravity's Rainbow*

Kurt Vonnegut *Slaughterhouse-Five: or, The Children's Crusade, A Duty-Dance with Death*

William Blake
British, 1757–1827
Christ Offers to Redeem Man, 1808
Illustration to John Milton's,
Paradise Lost
Pen and watercolor on paper
19½ x 15½ inches
Gift by subscription
90.94

Edouard Manet
French, 1832–1883
Frontispiece to Edgar Allen Poe's
The Raven (Le Corbeau), Paris, 1875
21½ x 14¼ inches
Gift of W. G. Russell Allen
M32799

BRITISH MYSTERIES: WRITERS AND THEIR SLEUTHS

Margery Allingham	Albert Campion
M. C. Beaton	Hamish Macbeth
Agatha Christie	Miss Marple
Colin Dexter	Chief Inspector Morse
Elizabeth George	Inspector Thomas Lynley
Martha Grimes	Inspector Richard Jury
Reginald Hill	Superintendent Dalziel and Peter Pascoe
P. D. James	Commander Adam Dalgliesh
Ngaio Marsh	Inspector Roderick Alleyn
Ellis Peters	Brother Cadfael
Ruth Rendell	Chief Inspector Wexford
Dorothy L. Sayers	Lord Peter Wimsey

"Do not expect to remember what you read....With a poor memory one can read The Thirty-Nine Steps *every ten years."*
Virginia Woolf

Edouard Manet
French, 1832–1883
"Open Here I Flung the Shutter"
Illustration to Edgar Allen Poe's
The Raven (Le Corbeau), Paris, 1875
Lithograph
15¾ x 11¾ inches
Gift of W. G. Russell Allen
32.466

AMERICAN MYSTERIES: WRITERS AND THEIR SLEUTHS

Lilian Jackson Braun	Jim Qwilleran and His Siamese Cats
James Lee Burke	Dave Robicheaux
Joyce Christmas	Lady Margaret Priam
Patricia Cornwell	Dr. Kay Scarpetta
Amanda Cross	Kate Fansler
Sue Grafton	Kinsey Millhone
Carolyn Hart	Annie Laurance
Joan Hess	Arly Hanks
Tony Hillerman	Joe Leaphorn
Ed McBain	Steve Carella
Charlotte McLeod	Sara Kelling
Walter Mosley	Easy Rawlins
Marcia Muller	Sharon McCone
Sara Paretsky	V. I. Warshawski
Robert B. Parker	Spenser
Nancy Pickard	Jenny Cain

Lilian Westcott Hale
American, 1881–1963
L'Edition de Luxe, 1910
Oil on canvas
23½ x 15 inches
Gift of Miss Mary C. Wheelwright
35.1487

GREAT CLASSIC ROMANCES

Charlotte Brontë *Jane Eyre*

Emily Brontë *Wuthering Heights*

F. Scott Fitzgerald *The Great Gatsby*

Gustave Flaubert *Madame Bovary*

John Fowles *The French Lieutenant's Woman*

Thomas Hardy *Tess of the d'Urbervilles*

D. H. Lawrence *Lady Chatterley's Lover*

Margaret Mitchell *Gone With the Wind*

Boris Pasternak *Doctor Zhivago*

Leo Tolstoy *Anna Karenina*

Edith Wharton *The Age of Innocence*

Muhammad 'Ali
Mughal or Deccan, about 1610
Thoughtful Man
Opaque watercolor on paper
10.1 x 11.8 cm
Francis Bartlett Donation of 1912 and Picture Fund
14.663

SPLENDID SERIES

E. F. Benson
Make Way for Lucia: The Complete Lucia

Robertson Davies
The Deptford Trilogy (Fifth Business, The Manticore, World of Wonders)

Lawrence Durrell
The Alexandria Quartet (Justine, Balthazar, Mountolive, Clea)

John Galsworthy
The Forsyte Saga (Man of Property, In Chancery, To Let, The White Monkey, The Silver Spoon, Swan Song)

Naguib Mahfouz
The Cairo Trilogy (Palace Walk, Palace of Desire, Sugar Street)

Patrick O'Brian
The Aubrey/Maturin novels (Master and Commander, Post Captain and *H. M. S. Surprise* are the first three.)

Edna O'Brien
The Country Girls Trilogy and *Epilogue*

Paul Scott
The Raj Quartet(The Jewel in the Crown, The Day of the Scorpion, The Towers of Silence, A Division of the Spoils)

Sigrid Undset
Kristin Lavransdatter (The Bridal Wreath, The Mistress of Husaby, The Cross)

Washington Allston
American, 1779–1843
The Poor Author and the Rich Bookseller, 1811
Oil on canvas
31 x 28 inches (78.7 x 71.1 cm)
Bequest of Charles Sprague Sargent
27.220

FOR LAUGHING OUT LOUD

Douglas Adams *The Hitchhiker's Guide to the Galaxy*

Patrick Dennis *Auntie Mame*

Gerald Durrell *My Family & Other Animals*

Joseph Heller *Catch–22*

Jerome K. Jerome *Three Men in a Boat*

David Lodge *Changing Places*

Peter Mayle *A Year in Provence*

Nancy Mitford *The Pursuit of Love & Love in a Cold Climate: Two Novels*

Farley Mowat *The Dog Who Wouldn't Be*

Eric Newby *A Short Walk in the Hindu Kush*

James Thurber *Thurber Carnival*

P. G. Wodehouse *Most of P. G. Wodehouse*

John Singer Sargent
American, 1856–1925
Simplon Pass: Reading, 1911
Watercolor
20 x 14 inches
Hayden Collection. Charles Henry Hayden Fund.
12.214

FAVORITES BY WOMEN AUTHORS

Isabel Allende *Eva Luna*

Maya Angelou *I Know Why the Caged Bird Sings*

Margaret Atwood *Surfacing*

Marguerite Duras *The Lover*

Laura Esquivel *Like Water for Chocolate*

Marilyn French *The Women's Room*

Ellen Gilchrist *Victory Over Japan: A Book of Stories*

Jamaica Kincaid *Annie John*

Barbara Kingsolver *The Bean Trees*

Doris Lessing *The Golden Notebook*

Tillie Olsen *Tell Me a Riddle*

Walter Crane
English, 1845–1915
"Tis their daughter, Princess Joan"
Illustration for Mary de Morgan's *The Heart of Princess Joan*
London, McMillan, 1880
Pencil
7⅛ x 5¼ inches
Gift of Mrs. Richard Cary Curtis
58.336

Kingsley Amis *Lucky Jim*

Harriet Doerr *Stones for Ibarra*

Louise Erdrich *Love Medicine: A Novel*

Ford Madox Ford *The Good Soldier*

Nadine Gordimer *Burger's Daughter*

John Irving *A Prayer for Owen Meany*

John Knowles *A Separate Peace*

Doris Lessing *The Summer Before the Dark*

Gabriel Garcia Marquez *One Hundred Years of Solitude*

Gloria Naylor *The Women of Brewster Place*

Richard Rodriguez *Hunger of Memory: The Education of Richard Rodriguez, an Autobiography*

Henry Roth *Call It Sleep*

Wole Soyinka *Aké: The Years of Childhood*

Muriel Spark *Memento Mori*

Amy Tan *The Joy Luck Club*

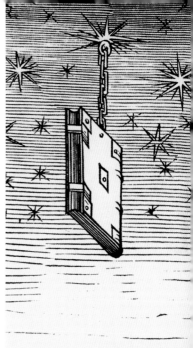

Hans Burgkmair
German, 1473–1531
"How the young White King
learns about medicine"
From Der Weisskunig
(manuscript)
Woodcut
8½ x 7¾ inches
William Francis Warden Fund
57.40

Harunobu
Japanese
A Girl Reading a Letter at Bedtime
Japanese Print, Hashirae
Spaulding Collection
21.4570

THE ARMCHAIR TRAVELLER

Elenore Smith Bowen *Return to Laughter*

Isak Dinesen *Out of Africa*

Lawrence Durrell *Bitter Lemons*

M. F. K. Fisher *Two Towns in Provence*

E. M. Forster *A Passage to India*

Graham Greene *The Heart of the Matter*

Ernest Hemingway *A Moveable Feast*

Peter Matthiessen *The Snow Leopard*

Alan Moorehead *The White Nile*

Mary Morris *Nothing to Declare*

Eric Newby *A Book of Travellers' Tales*

Paul Theroux *The Old Patagonian Express*

"Their lips were four red roses on a stalk,
Which in their summer beauty kissed each other"

Richard III., Act iv. Sc 3

Walter Crane
English, 1845–1915
Illustration from *Flowers from Shakespeare's Garden,*
A Posy from the Plays
London, Castell & Co., 1906
Lithograph
10 x 7½ inches
Bequest of W. G. Russell Allen
63.731

CAPTIVATING SHORT STORIES

Jorge Luis Borges *Labyrinths: Selected Short Stories & Other Writings*

Elizabeth Bowen *The Collected Stories of Elizabeth Bowen*

Raymond Carver *Where I'm Calling From: New and Selected Stories*

John Cheever *The Stories of John Cheever*

Andre Dubus *Selected Stories of Andre Dubus*

William Faulkner *Collected Stories of William Faulkner*

Flannery O'Connor *Complete Stories*

Katherine Anne Porter *The Collected Stories of Katherine Anne Porter*

Isaac Bashevis Singer *The Collected Stories of Isaac Bashevis Singer*

Eudora Welty *The Collected Stories of Eudora Welty*

Puss conversed with the Ogre, who said that he could
Assume any shape that he chose - bad or good
great or small - as he'd show & the Ogre so slvery
Turned into a mouse & was swallowed by pussy
At this moment his Majesty's carriage
Puss hurried downstairs, was heard
At the door flung wide open, appeared
before they could
ring.

Walter Crane
English, 1845–1915
"Puss Welcomes the King, the Princess, and his Master"
Illustration to *Puss in Boots*
Pen, ink, and watercolor
8 x 6⅛ inches
Gift of Mrs. John L. Gardner
92.2575

A CHILDREN'S STARTER LIBRARY

One year

Margaret Wise Brown *Goodnight Moon*

Eric Hill *Where's Spot?*

Helen Oxenbury *Tickle, Tickle*

Jack Prelutsky *Read-Aloud Rhymes for the Very Young*

Two years

Eric Carle *The Very Hungry Caterpillar*

Bruce Degan *Jamberry*

Bill Martin *Brown Bear, Brown Bear, What Do You See?*

Beatrix Potter *The Tale of Peter Rabbit*

Three years

H. A. Rey *Curious George*

Michael Rosen *We're Going on a Bear Hunt*

Dr. Seuss *The Cat in the Hat*

Charlotte Voake *Three Little Pigs and Other Favorite Nursery Stories*

Four years

Virginia Lee Burton *Mike Mulligan & His Steam Shovel*

Don Freeman *Corduroy*

Robert McCloskey *Make Way for Ducklings*

Maurice Sendak *Where the Wild Things Are*

Five years

Patricia Polacco *Mrs. Katz & Tush*

William Steig *Brave Irene*

Bernard Waber *Ira Sleeps Over*

Vera B. Williams *A Chair for My Mother*

Edward Burne Jones
English, 1833–98
Cinderella
Watercolor and gouache on paper
26⅜ x 12⅜ inches
Anonymous gift in memory
of Charlotte Beebe Wilbour, 1932
32.409

Pablo Picasso
Spanish, 1881–1973
The Cat
From Buffon, *Histoire Naturelle*
Paris, Martin Fabiani, 1942
Etching and aquatint
14¾ x 11¼ inches
Bequest of W. G. Russell Allen
63.751

CHILDREN'S BOOKS TOO GOOD TO MISS

Louisa May Alcott *Little Women*

Frances H. Burnett *The Secret Garden*

Betsy Byars *The Summer of the Swans*

Lewis Carroll *Alice's Adventures in Wonderland*

Louise Fitzhugh *Harriet the Spy*

Shelby Foot *Shiloh*

Jean Craighead George *My Side of the Mountain*

Kenneth Grahame *The Wind in the Willows*

Patricia MacLachlan *Sarah, Plain and Tall*

A. A. Milne *Winnie-the-Pooh*

Scott O'Dell *Island of the Blue Dolphins*

Katherine Paterson *Bridge to Terabithia*

Elizabeth George Speare *The Witch of Blackbird Pond*

Suzanne Fisher Staples *Shabanu: Daughter of the Wind*

Robert Louis Stevenson *Treasure Island*

J. R. R. Tolkien *The Hobbit*

Mark Twain *The Adventures of Tom Sawyer*

E. B. White *Charlotte's Web*

Walter Crane
English, 1845–1915
The King is borne away
by the Wicked Fairy of the Desert
from *The Yellow Dwarf*
London and New York, John Lane
Wood engraving
10¾ x 7⅛ inches
Anonymous gift

IRRESISTIBLE SERIES
FOR CHILDREN

Lloyd Alexander *"Land of Prydain"* series

Beverly Cleary *Ramona the Pest* series

C. S. Lewis *The Chronicles of Narnia* series

L. M. Montgomery *Anne of Green Gables* series

Laura Ingalls Wilder *Little House on the Prairie* series

Master of the Boccaccio Illustrations
Netherlands, 15th century
"Adam and Eve," from Giovanni Boccaccio's
La Ruine des Nobles Hommes et Femmes,
Bruges, C. Mansion, 1476
Hand–colored engraving
7⅜ x 6¾ inches
Maria Antoinette Evans Fund
32.458

PRINTS AND DRAWINGS

The Department of Prints and Drawings at the
Museum of Fine Arts, Boston considers books
illustrated by printmakers to be an integral part of
the print collection. The rare book collection
comprises more than 5,000 illustrated volumes,
dating from the fifteenth century to the present day.

The Bruges edition of Boccaccio's tale of the
downfall of famous men and women (some legendary,
some real) was the first printed book to be illustrated
with engravings. The Museum's copy is one of three
known examples in which all nine engraved
illustrations have been pasted in, and the only copy
in which all engravings have been colored by hand,
giving the intended effect of illuminated miniatures.

Master of the Boccaccio
Illustrations
Netherlands, 15th century
from Giovanni Boccaccio's
*La Ruine des Nobles Hommes
et Femmes*,
Bruges, C. Mansion, 1476
Hand–colored engraving
7⅜ x 6¾ inches
Maria Antoinette Evans Fund
32.458

Anonymous
Italian, 16th century
St. John the Evangelist
From *Epistole e Evangeli Volgari*, Venice, 1522
Woodcut
6 x 6 inches
Gift of Philip Hofer
51.1940

BOOKS LENT

BOOKS LENT

BOOKS LENT

BOOKS LENT

Anonymous
Italian, 16th century
Portrait of the Author
From Bernardino Corio, *Patria Historia*, Milan, 1503
11⅛ x 6⅛ inches
William A. Sargent Fund
46.467

BOOKS LENT

Books Lent

Anonymous
Swiss, 16th century
Illustration from Maynus de Mayneriis',
Dialogus Creaturarum Moralisatus
(Animal Dialogues with a moral turn),
Geneva, Jean Belot, 1500
Woodcut
2⅜ x 4¹³⁄₁₆ inches
William Francis Warden Fund
53.17

BOOKS GIVEN AS GIFTS

BOOKS GIVEN AS GIFTS

Con li infideli perche fie fopreffo,
Chi con el catiuo homo fe nutrica
Dice Gregorio conuien che catiua
Sua uita facia e con effo inimica.
Quando del cane fu la forza priua
El fuo fignofe gli tolfe la fpica
Al catiuo feruir cofi fe ariua.
          Dunqȝ ciafchun che ufua
Se guardi da feruir allo inimico
Perche gli tole de la gloria il fpico
  ⸿De Sylua & leporibus.   Fabula; xxx,

Anonymous
Italian, 15th century
Of Frogs and Hares
From Aesop's *Fables*, Venice, 1497
4⅝ x 4¼ inches Woodcut
Special Print Fund and Harvey D. Parker Fund
54.1788

BOOKS GIVEN AS GIFTS

Teſtudo prona.

Testudo supina.

D.iii.

Pierre Belon
French, 1517–1564
"Sea Turtle" from *De Aquatilibus*
Paris, Charles Etienne, 1553
Hand–colored woodcut
4⅛ x 6⅔ inches
Gift of Arthur and Charlotte Vershbow
1989.844

BOOKS GIVEN AS GIFTS

BOOKS TO READ

BOOKS TO READ

J. M. Moreau le jeune inv.   J. B. Simonet Sculp. 1778.

La nature étaloit à nos yeux toute sa magnificence,

Emil. T. 2. Pag. 8.

J. B. Simonet (after J. M. Moreau)
French, 1742–1813
Illustration from J. J. Rousseau's
"Emil ou de l' Education"
London, 1774
Engraving
7 x 5⅛ inches
William A. Sargent Collection
37.1734

BOOKS TO READ

James Caldwall, after Philip Reinagle (1749–1833)
English, 1739–1819
The Blue Passion Flower, 1800
From Thornton, *The Temple of Flora or Garden of Nature*
Aquatint, stipple and line engraving, printed
in color and hand colored
Bequest of Estate of George P. Dike, Elita R. Dike Collection
69.308

BOOKS TO READ

No. 254
VILLAGE LIBRARY.

Beauties in vain their pretty eyes may roll;
Charms strike the sense, but merit wins the soul.

Anonymous
American, 19th century
The Village Library, Farmington, Connecticut
Engraved bookplate
M. and M. Karolik Collection
41.678

BALZAC ILLUSTRÉ.

LA
PEAU DE CHAGRIN.

ÉTUDES SOCIALES.

PARIS.

H. DELLOYE,   VICTOR LECOU,

ÉDITEURS,

Rue des Filles-Saint-Thomas, 13, place de la Bourse.

1838.

Frontispiece from
Balzac's *La Peau de Chagrin*
Paris. 1838
10¼ x 6¼ inches
William A. Sargent Collection
37.2457

Anonymous
American, 19th century
The Book Bindery
Pencil and watercolor
6 x 8⅞ inches
M. and M. Karolik Collection
58.835

W. H. Hooper (after Edward
Burne-Jones)
English, 19th century
Illustration from *The Works of
Geoffrey Chaucer*,
London, Kelmscott Press, 1896
Woodcut
15 x 10¼ inches
William A. Sargent Collection
Book Reg. 2894

The tendre croppes, and the yonge sonne
Hath in the Ram his halfe cours yronne,
And smale foweles maken melodye,
That slepen al the nyght with open eye,
So priketh hem nature in hir corages;
Thanne longen folk to goon on pilgrimages,
And palmeres for to seken straunge strondes,
To ferne halwes, kowthe in sondry londes;
And specially, from every shires ende
Of Engelond, to Caunterbury they wende,
The hooly blisful martir for to seke,
That hem hath holpen whan that they were
    seeke.

BIFIL that in that seson on a day,
In Southwerk at the Tabard as
    I lay,
Redy to wenden on my pilgrym-
    age
To Caunterbury with ful devout
corage,
At nyght were come into that hostelrye
Wel nyne and twenty in a compaignye,
Of sondry folk, by aventure yfalle
In felaweshipe, and pilgrimes were they alle,
That toward Caunterbury wolden ryde.

s soote
ced to the roote,
h licour,
e flour;
ete breeth
heeth

BOOKS TO READ

BOOKS TO READ

Aubrey Beardsley
English, 1872–1898
Illustration from Sir Thomas Malory's *Le Morte D'Arthur*
London, William Caxton, 1893–1894
Woodcut
3 x 1½ inches
William A. Sargent Collection
Book Reg. 2390

BOOKS TO READ

BOOKS TO READ

BOOKS TO READ

Pierre Bonnard
French, 1867–1947
"Danse," from *Petites Scènes Familières*
Lithograph
13¹¹⁄₁₆ x 6⅞ inches
Lee M. Friedman Fund
66.368

BOOKS TO READ

W. Holman Hunt
English, 1827–1910
Lady of Shalott, for Alfred Tennyson's *Poems*
London, Edward Moxon, 1857
Wood engraving on India paper, proof
9⅞ x 7½ inches
John H. and Ernestine A. Payne Fund
55.1349

BOOKS TO READ

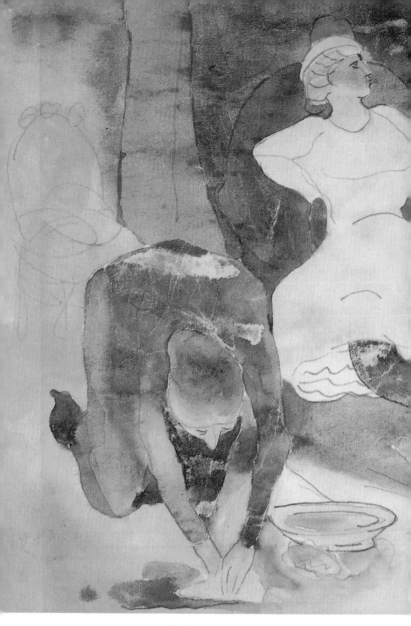

Charles Demuth
American, 1892–1935
Illustration No. 8 for Zola's *Nana*, (Chapter XIII), 1915–1916
Watercolor over graphite
7⅞ x 11⅝ inches
Hayden Collection. Charles Henry Hayden Fund
58.30

107

PHONE NUMBERS AND HOURS
FOR LIBRARIES AND
BOOKSTORES

Phone Numbers and Hours
for Libraries and Bookstores

Phone Numbers and Hours
for Libraries and Bookstores